Lenten Lent

Lenten Lent

A Way to Refresh & Renew Your Spirit

Donna Schaper

Editor: Michael Schwartzentruber
Cover and Interior: Cyrus Gandevia
Proofreader: Dianne Greenslade
Cover image: Feisal Somji

Unless otherwise noted, scripture quotations are from the *New Revised Standard Version* of the Bible, copyright 1983, Division of Christian Education of the National Council of Churches of Christ in the United States of America. All rights reserved. Used by permission.

 WoodLake is an imprint of Wood Lake Publishing, Inc. Wood Lake Publishing acknowledges the financial support of the Government of Canada through the Canada Book Fund (CBF) for its publishing activities. Wood Lake Publishing also acknowledges the financial support of the Province of British Columbia through the Book Publishing Tax Credit.

At Wood Lake Publishing, we practise what we publish, being guided by a concern for fairness, justice, and equal opportunity in all of our relationships with employees and customers. Wood Lake Publishing is committed to caring for the environment and all creation. Wood Lake Publishing recycles, reuses, and encourages readers to do the same. Resources are printed on 100% post-consumer recycled paper and more environmentally friendly groundwood papers (newsprint), whenever possible. A percentage of all profit is donated to charitable organizations.

Library and Archives Canada Cataloguing in Publication

Schaper, Donna, author
     Lenten Lent : a way to refresh & renew your spirit / Donna Schaper.

Issued in print and electronic formats.
ISBN 978-1-77064-793-0 (pbk.).--ISBN 978-1-77064-796-1 (epub)

     1. Lent--Meditations. 2. Lent--Prayers and devotions.
I. Title.

BV85.S33 2015   242'.34   C2014-907152-3
                                        C2014-907153-1

Published by Woodlake
An imprint of Wood Lake Publishing Inc.
485 Beaver Lake Road, Kelowna, BC, Canada, V4V 1S5
www.woodlakebooks.com
250.766.2778

Printing 10 9 8 7 6 5 4 3 2 1
Printed in Canada

Table of Contents

Introduction

Appropriate spiritual technology

If you are like me, you long for an appropriately-sized spiritual technology, one that can renew you and bring you to new life. You want it to be *simple* in an elegant way, like the right vase for the right flowers. And you want it to be *elegant* in a simple way, like the way a pair of scissors re-usably presents itself on the right occasion.

If you are like me, you long for spiritual methods, practices, measurements – ways to travel that long way to God. You don't want anything fancy so much as you want something just right. You don't want to waste time or energy so much as to *use* time and energy in a renewable and renewing way.

I have also cried with longing, looking for a broom. Just to clean up the hallway. Some days I even cry that I don't have *time* to sweep the porch or the deck. It would be so lovely if I could. And I can't. Because I can't find the broom, or the time. Those of us who live deep in the time famine understand. On my recent vacation, staying at a friend's house, I swept her front porch with vigour every morning. It was my feast and my vacation. At home, my porch is a mess.

And then there's the dustpan. I don't know why it keeps changing its residence, but it does.

And the fingernail clippers. They never seem to be in my suitcase at the right time or, when I am home, they usually seem to be in my suitcase – the one I just put down in the cellar.

I reserve my deepest praise for the shopping cart that allows me to go shopping for groceries in New York and to buy the five pound bag of flour instead of the two pounder. I usually save about two dollars a pound on this exchange. My backpack often strains my back, so heavy does it get while I am carrying the too-much of my days.

Each of these technologies gives me freedom from the car. And yes, today I bought a new Prius. My sixth, actually. I love my Prius. It allows me to get *out* of town. But even more, I love my pockets and my shopping carts. They allow me to stay *in* town. I need freedom and I need motion and, yes, I am a card carrying member of the First World and its fantasies of abundance.

In these meditations, I devote myself again to renewal, not *just* for me, but surely for me. And not *just* for you, but surely for you. And not *just* for our communities, but surely for them as well. I am looking for an appropriate spiritual technology, a method and a way to renew my spirit when it gets lost near the dustpan. A daily devotional is as good as any broom or scissors. It lets our days end, knowing we have at least tried to notice time and tempo as they pass through our hours on this earth.

Perhaps if you read this guide, we will be together. Or at least we will reach for each other and help each other find appropriate technologies for whatever tasks our spirits have to face. Would it be too much to hope for the elegance of simplicity? Or the mutuality of engagement? Or to hope that your people might become my people, and my people become your people? Your family my family, and my family your family? Your neighbour my neighbour, and my neighbour yours? Perhaps your problems will become my problems and my problems your problems? Your emissions my emissions and my emissions yours? Dare we hope for a spiritual miracle of sorts? That your resurrection into joy will be mine as well, and my resurrection yours?

May we feast in the time it will take us to renew ourselves this Lent. May we find the largest Zest of all in the divine seasonality of all life. May we find a way to renewing prayer, energizing action, and therein devote ourselves to a devotional life that does not deplete us but instead fills us.

Ultimately, it is my hope that these devotions will accompany you through Lent and yield a harvest of solar and wind energy in you. By solar I mean a sunnier disposition and by wind I mean something like wind in your sails. Renewable energy is not just material in form. It is also metaphoric, metaphysical, and very hard to measure with scales or rulers. May these 40 meditations be a handful of hope to guide you on that journey.

Guidelines for Small Groups

You may want to use the simple technology of the daily devotional all by yourself. You may find its individual practice just right for evoking the solitude in you. On the other hand, you may want a companion or two, along your renewing way. You may already be part of a book club or a Bible-study group or a coffee klatch and want to renew with these friends at your side. If you want to bring a small group together during Lent, think of these options. Think of them as guidelines not rules. Think of them as trail markers, like the white blaze on the tree in the wood that keeps you on the path.

1. Set a time and place. Four sessions would allow for ten devotionals a day to be considered. Or you may want something weekly during the period of Lent. Make the time easy – like breakfast Mondays, or lunch Tuesdays, or dinner Thursdays. Before or after church on Sundays can be an easy time if you want the group to be open and include those who can only come once or twice. A closed group makes for greater intimacy of sharing; an open group makes for less intimacy but has the advantage of greater diversity and attendance possibilities.

2. If people have children, figure out how to rotate childcare or pay for it. If people need transportation, figure out how to travel together or car pool. If you need food, rotate the responsibility for bringing it and making it – and cleaning it up. Be sure there is a leader each time you meet. Make sure he or she knows how to lead. Rotating leadership gives everybody a turn and everybody some practice at leading. If your pastor wants to lead, surely let him or her do that. In other words,

make sure somebody is in charge of sharing the airtime and make sure that person has permission to lead. Rotate hosts for each event so that somebody is first to arrive and greet, and last to leave and lock up. Make the appropriate spiritual technology also very practical. When details get in the way of the program, watch out. But without attention to details, the space won't clear for the spiritually renewing experience.

3. Decide on whether you are going to focus on the meditations, the scriptures, the prayers, or the action steps. Or you may want to find the metaphors and images throughout and focus on them, as elegant simplicity for yourself during Lent. Which images work for you? Which don't? In other words, take a bite of these pages of 40 days. Don't get spiritual indigestion.

4. Make sure the space is safe for disagreement and exchange that might be volatile. Don't expect every day to satisfy every person. Acknowledge that renewal and refreshment may involve some personal engagement and group conflict – not the mean kind but the kind that forces us to the ground of our being. That ground will not be the same for all people.

5. Begin with prayer and end with prayer, even if it is just a time to be really quiet.

6. Have an anniversary of the group next Lent. See if anything changed.

Daily Devotions

1. "For I am fearfully and wonderfully made..."
~ Psalm 139:14

Sometimes we find ourselves saying, "My get up and go has got up and went." Others say, "I am so tired of being tired." Still others declare that there is no vacation time long enough to recover an imagined previous energy. In the middle of these multiple fatigues – of body, spirit, culture, and capacity – we allow the exhaustion to Lenten us. Lent is not a verb, of course. It is a noun, a time of lengthening into the trouble we try so hard to suppress. This Lent let us lengthen into cultural and personal exhaustion. Then let us renew and rise.

How can we frame the question of energy in such a way as to be gentle to our fatigue while also combatting it? How can we Lenten it? How can we lift it off the shelf of suppression and repression onto the great table of renewal and resurrection? Can we be both tired *and* renewable, even long after we don't believe in our own renewal?

I believe yes. The answer is prayer. Prayer is not as big an item as people imagine it to be. Prayer is more like a pause than anything else. It is blessed reflection that follows excessive action.

Like solar and wind energy, prayer is a source of renewable energy, reminding us that we are fearfully and wonderfully made. Imagine renewal. Let the imagining be a form of renewal. Picture yourself as fearfully and wonderfully made.

Prayer: Renewing God, when we are too tired to pray, let us just pause and in the pause fill us with mysterious energy. Let the trouble come to us. Let us feel it long enough and deep enough to tend it. Let us let Lent Lenten us. Amen.

Action step: Renew your interest in prayer. Take a breath before you eat, learn to sigh when you are tired. Become someone with a prayer practice, one who knows you are just practicing. Do you need a prayer rug? Or a prayer notebook? Or a place where you always pray, even if it is only at the first red light you pass on your way out of work or to work every day? Find a "thing," like your toothbrush, or a place on your daily route. Let it remind you to pray.

2. "Save me, O God, by your name."
~ Psalm 54:1

We often say with a tiny bit of defensiveness, "I am doing what I can." It's very hard to do what you can't. One of the problems with canning all you can, a joke from the Ball Jar Company, is that we often count our capacity and incapacity as limited. We do what we can with what we have, and we don't do what we cannot with what we don't have. We imagine a kind of fixed sum of energy.

I often think of energy as renewable. If I have a good talk with someone, I can be energized by it. If I have a hard talk with someone, I can be de-energized. I see prayer as a kind of talk with God, even if it is only a hum, or a sigh, or a redirection. A hum prays calm. A sigh prays sadness. A redirection can keep you from writing that email and relieves you of the notion that you have to do something about everything. Invoking the name of God, even if it is "OH GAWD" or "oh god," can renew your energy.

Many of us use a "sit spot" as a substitute for prayer that uses words. There may just be too many words and too little sitting. A sit spot is simply a convenient place that you return to frequently to sit. A sit spot teaches you how to look at the same tree over and

over, or at the same picture over and over. It insists on a pause from action into the pause of reflection. Being saved by the name of God, available in a hum or a sigh or a redirection or a sit spot, can renew you. Keeping distance from the name of God can weaken you.

Prayer: Holy Spirit, you with the really good name, draw near and teach us habits that renew us. Let us just sit with our stuff and, from that sitting, rise and renew. Amen.

Action step: Locate a place that has your name on it. Maybe it is a hotel lobby you can borrow from time to time. Or a good chair in your house in a good corner with the best *feng shui* and quietest view. Or maybe it is a bowl of water in your office into which you dip your tired hands from time to time during the day. Use that place regularly and make it your own. When you go there, remember the renewable you. Pray for yourself there. Pray for others in other places. In your sit spot, pray for you. Get to know yourself there.

3. "Lord, he whom you love is ill."
~ John 11:3

Depression is a matter that stands in the way of renewal, recycling, and resurrection. Severe depression kills off people in small and large ways. Sometimes it comes in a daily nagging; other times in real suicide, the kind that prohibits any more days from coming. If we don't face it, there will be no renewal, only a repeat. The good news is we *can* face it, whether it is big or small, nagging or a deeper never-mind.

I write this as the apparent suicide of Robin Williams is hitting the news. By the time you read it, his death at 63 will be old news.

Some new tragedy will have taken its place, making this a great day to think about illness as a matter of the soul as well as of the body. This very day many people will be wondering whether life is worth living and they won't have the accompaniment of wealth or comedy or notoriety. They will wonder why life is uphill both ways. They will wonder why they bother. They will think about ending it all as a better option than another today-like tomorrow.

Illness has been diminished to matters of the body, in the same way so much of life is diminished to matters material and biological. Material-*ism* is something we love to complain about it. Today, let us sophisticate our complaint. Let us realize that mental illness is real and that people who take their own life do so to escape extraordinary pain, pain that is with them at the breakfast they can't eat, the lunch which looks like mush, the dinner they see with vacant eyes – eyes deeply turned inside. Mental illness, like soul fatigue, causes people to use guns on school children, bombs on buildings, ropes on themselves, and to try one pill after another. Soul fatigue is illness, too, and it is *not* a sin.

As Lent lentens us, let us not blame but instead learn to love.

Prayer: Bring us to a place beyond judgment and its canny distance from what hurts. Restore compassion to our "health" "care" systems. Pull down our wagging finger and open our hearts. Amen.

Action step: Move beyond shame and blame, and their waste of energy. Become a recycler of trouble. Let trouble become your teacher and sadness your sage. When you start to beat yourself up, stop. Turn. Let your own soul fatigue, recognized and realized, become the source of your renewed energy. Realize that worry gets you nowhere, absolutely nowhere at all. And if you must be down, give the sadness a time limit.

4. "While you have the light, believe in the light, so that you may become children of light."
~ John 12:36

Someone smart said, "It has to be seen to be believed and believed to be seen." So many of us have seen the light, but don't let it affect our identity or our habits of seeing. We have a *little* hope when we could have a *lot*.

God is active in people's lives, if we just pay attention. Paying attention is easier than you think. It is at least a two-step process. It means actively withdrawing attention from life's persistent irritants, which include (usually) members of our own family or congregation. Then it means shining our flashlight on life's persistent encouragement, which includes (usually) members of our own family, or congregation, or community as well. It means turning the channel on the radio station to listen to some music we enjoy. It means withdrawing oxygen from the crap of life and oxygenating the beauties. Becoming a child of the light is a choice about what to see. It can become a habit.

How will you know if you are renewing? You will know because you are lighter. Light is not just the opposite of dark. It is also the opposite of heavy. We don't have to dislike the dark to become light. Instead we can move the heavy aside.

Becoming lighter also means engaging our inner mystic. When we live lightly, we see new heavens and new earths everywhere. Those whose cynicism has caused them to eat the seeds on the bottom of the birdcage do not weigh us down. We sing. We fly. We eat out of the bird feeder.

Jesus seems to think we have a choice about whether to choose light or heaviness. I think he is right.

Prayer: O God, change the climate in our hearts and in our souls so that we can not only *see* the light, but *believe* in it and *experience* it and let it *become* who we are. Amen.

Action step: Go on a spiritual diet. Lighten up. Find a way to leave some of your baggage home and put a dance in your step. Use music if you have to. You can lose weight.

5. "A leper came to him begging him, and kneeling he said to him, "If you choose, you can make me clean."
~ Mark 1:40

The leper may have had that dreadful disease of leprosy, but he was also full of trust. If you have ever wanted for trust, you might even be jealous of his skin condition. Much of our trouble has its source in not being able to trust that anything can be different, or that *we* can be different. Hoping to trust again is what reflection and a sit spot can bring you. You may find that you have sat long enough with your trouble and that you are ready to stand up. A Lenten spiritual practice may be nothing more than permission to sit through our stuff long enough that we are willing to rise from it. A little trust can go a long way towards the rising. A smart theologian said that the gospel is nothing more than the permission and the commandment to enter difficulty with hope. You sit with the difficulty long enough to transcend it. In other words, you can't go around the difficulty; you have to go through it.

Being bereft of trust is an acute kind of poverty. Losing hope is even harder. Hope is the prelude to trust. Not being able to trust rivals the worst of diseases and, in fact, is a dis-ease or an absence of ease itself. Our world has made astonishing medical progress

with formerly incurable diseases like leprosy. We haven't done as well with trust.

I think of an important article in a recent edition of *The New York Times*, called "A World in Denial of What it Knows," by Geoffrey Wheatcroft. Wheatcroft takes on the matter of trust and argues that today's biggest dis-ease is not knowing what we in fact know. He reminds us of the famous, if gnomic, saying by Donald H. Rumsfeld, then the U.S. Secretary of Defense, that there are "known knowns…[and] there are known unknowns. There are also unknown unknowns." Wheatcroft argues our malaise is due to none of the above. It is, instead, caused by "Unknown knowns." What he means is something different than denial or evasion. "Unknown knowns are things… which are easily knowable, or indeed known, but which people choose to unknow." We preferred, for example, to not know that boom often relates to bust. We preferred to think that the war in Iraq would not cost us much. "The calamities that followed the invasion of Iraq were not only foreseeable, they were also foreseen." He continues, "What kind of willful obtusity ever suggested that subprime mortgages were a good idea? An intelligent child would have known that there is no good time to lend money to people who can obviously never repay it." He does not attend to global warming in this piece, although he could have. We *do* know. Nor does he address the lost generation of Protestantism, a truth that most readers of this devotional do know. Nor does he address what happens if we skip the full yoga or gym workout with a kind of predictable regularity. In the "unknown knowns," we just choose not to know, in an astonishing absence of trust in our own judgment.

We know the pain of not trusting. We also know the pain of self-deception. We want renewal, redemption, even resurrection.

We even know how to achieve these renewable forms of energy. Spiritual practice that gets rid of stale energy – in the home, in the bowel, in the daily deliverables – that's how.

Prayer: Maybe you shouldn't have trusted us with so much, O God, but you did. Help us to return the favour. Amen.

Action step: Make a list of all the things and people you don't trust and choose one of them. Change your point of view. Trust the possibility that you were wrong about them, or it. Try again.

6. "But as for that good soil...it bears fruit."
~ Luke 8:15, Author's paraphrase

I went to a real church supper in a church that had a real kitchen, in Conway, Massachusetts. The occasion was the rededication of the sanctuary after a mould outbreak had shut the place down for three years. The mould outbreak was followed by a flood of the newly refurbished kitchen and downstairs. The small-but-mighty congregation not only survived but flourished under these multiple curses – and in spite of the 5000 volunteer hours, plus serious mould removal professionals, it took to create their lovely new space.

The reason I will remember the supper is not just that it started at 5:30, before our office even closes in NYC. Or that the pork loin, apples with cinnamon, sweet potatoes, mixed vegetables, and berry crisp with whipped cream were not splendid. They were. The reason I will remember this church supper above all the rest is that the neighbouring church, the Montague church, prepared the supper for the Conway church. They also cleaned up the inaugural dishes.

The band from the local Catholic Church led the music during the worship. A reverse offering was taken. "You have endured so much for so long that we are not asking for another nickel. Instead, we invite you to enjoy this chocolate."

We usually do brunch in restaurants in our neighbourhood of New York City and don't have a kitchen, unless you call a sink and a refrigerator and an island in a corner a kitchen, which I do not. We call it the "little kitchen that could," and now I know the little church that could, and did, and can too.

Prayer: O God, thanks for neighbours who know how to be neighbourly. Remind us how much ordinary people can do for themselves and for each other. Teach us to revere self-reliance, self-governance, and the sharing economy. Amen.

Action step: Do something for one of your neighbours that you don't have to do. Surprise them. Recycle your energy in another place, with other people. You will find replenishment.

7. "Jonah was in the belly of the fish for three days."
~ Jonah 1:17

I have never been in the belly of a whale, but I have often felt enclosed, eaten up, devoured with a lot of no-exit-sign kind of feelings. They happen in mundane ways, even though there is nothing mundane about the way most of us live in a time famine. That time famine results from a combination of overstimulation, stupid economies that cause commuting on behalf of real estate, and dumbed down work on behalf of other people's profits – each joined by the way we can't imagine how *not* to participate in them.

My time management consultant told me I needed a junk drawer, a place to put everything that I didn't know what to do about. I wanted to tell her that I'd need a half dozen drawers, not just one. Then I realized she was pushing me to focus on what was really important. Again, the road to the important is paved with detours. All that being said, I have decided to try softer, not harder, to find the still life. There is a picture above my desk that has a lovely still life in it. Mine is an unstill life. Perhaps a junk drawer is my way out of the belly of the whale. That way I'd have more time to imagine a different, more humane economy. Strikes me as important, right?

Prayer: O God, when we feel devoured by detail, give us a new thought and let us put all the old ones in the junk drawer. Amen.

Action step: Organize your junk drawer. Then organize your spiritual junk drawer. And then let the cleanup, internally and externally, be renewing.

8. "Do not put...God to the test."
~ Luke 4:12

This week is the 40th anniversary of my ordination. I know you imagine me too young and vigorous to have been gathering dust so long. But there it is. Tucson, Arizona, 40 years ago. I am having a lot of fun thinking about it, especially when I preach at other people's ordinations.

My latest ordinand was brilliant in her Ruth robe, laced with lace. The other women in the procession were equally splendid, one dressed in a very nicely fitted robe from Clergy Couture. She also wore pearls with her stole. A third woman was wearing a stole

her mother had made, out of fabric from her grandmother's dresses and her own. It was a mixture of calico and lace. On it was an owl. Why? The daughter had told the mother the story of the owl she had seen in the forest; her stitching mother found it meaningful and fixed it in fabric.

If that perplexing word queer means anything, it means gender bending. It means becoming a minister after so many years of being a "woman minister." It also means feminists in lace and older women in sensible shoes. What fun it has been to be out of place for so long.

So many people say women don't belong in the ministry. They also accuse male clergy of being "effeminate," those guys in skirts, up in the stands with the women and girls while the real men play the real game on the field. One thing I have loved about ministry is how androgynous it is: if the women are too masculine and the men too feminine, isn't that wonderful?

Prayer: Thank you, God-who-is-beyond-male-and-female, always transgendering, draw near, and thank you, thank you, thank you. God of lepers and liars, you who are larger than mistakes and even malfeasance, come close and wrangle some truth out of us, before it is too late for us to live a life of trust. Give us the gift of one small turn of the key that will unlock us every day. Amen.

Action step: Pay a little attention to your gender today. Ask yourself if it is freeing you or failing you, or a little of both. Pay attention to what seems fixed in your life and fix it. If you want to do something queer, do it. Every step out of a small box is a step into a spacious life.

9. "After some days Paul said to Barnabas, 'Come, let us return and visit the believers in every city where we proclaimed the word of the Lord and see how they are doing.'"
~ Acts 15:36

Evaluation can renew you. There is nothing like an evaluation to shake things up. Paul and Barnabas are doing a review. They are taking the risk of looking back. If you love something enough, like the gospel, you won't dare be unaccountable to it. If you are a family, you'll want to keep a budget and evaluate whether you stick to it. If you are a business, you'll want to know if you are making money. If you are a school, you'll want to know if students are learning. If you are a congregation, you will count. You will count new members and whether they had "stickiness" a few years after their arrival. You will count pledges and whether any of them increased over time. You will count attendance and be aware of who came, and who didn't come back. You will notice if the parents who trusted you with their five-year-old still trust you with their seven-year-old.

If you made New Year's resolutions, this Lent would be a good time to remember them. Did you do what you said you would do? If not, why not? Where is the energy for them? Did it dissipate or did it increase? Do you need to repent the way you allowed your energy to dissipate?

Evaluation and accountability often have bad reputations. We dread them, mostly because people who don't have our best interests in mind so often use them against us.

Imagine something more joyful. Imagine welcoming a review of your congregation or yourself. Imagine being a partner in setting the criteria for that review with someone you trust. Imagine the faith it takes to try something different and to say, by the grace of God, "What we're doing isn't working." "What I tried, failed." "What I thought would happen didn't happen." Imagine the freedom that comes from really committing to something, so much so that you wouldn't think of failing at it. Or knowing that if failure came, you had the permission and the responsibility to try again a different way.

One of the things that Paul and Barnabas were spreading around was good news. It was the good news that, in Jesus, we could trust God's love to surround us. That surely means nearly constant assessment and reassessment of how things are going for us and for our communities. As individuals, many of us would like to become more free over time, even more joyous. To do so, we have to be less afraid of mistakes than we are of accountability. As congregations, many of us have seen numbers that shout that something we are doing isn't working. As individuals and as congregations, we often need new criteria for success. Numbers tell us one story; the spirit in the conversation in a coffee hour tells us another. When we make the important journey that Paul and Barnabas undertook, we may do so eagerly. We may face whatever we have to face. Then we recommit to a spread of love and freedom and joy. And next year, or at our next evaluation, we see how far we got towards those gospel goals and gifts.

Prayer: O God, if we are fried around the edges by too many reviews that were too trivial, re-engage us in the kind of review you would want for us. Show us the way to a joyous accountability to your promises. Amen.

Action step: Name the five things on which you would like God to evaluate you. Do a self-evaluation. Use a silly scale, like 1 to

5, and rate yourself. Then choose the highest mark you have and congratulate yourself for it. Then choose the lowest and do one thing that might make a difference to you…and to God.

10. What a Friend We Have in Jesus
~ Hymn title

For this Lenten journey, I advise finding friends to help you go where you want to go. Friends are the real recyclable. Note: People who find a walking or exercise partner walk or exercise. Duh. People who want to find a renewable and renewing energy need a partner just as much.

Time spent with friends or with an institution can help renew you. Institutions can be like friends; they can provide a community from which you can evoke the spiritually renewable you. Maybe your religious institution isn't helping you? Find a new one, even if you decide to stick with the old one as well.

Choosing the right institution as your Jesus friend is very practical. It is a little like what we know about exercise. The exercise that will work for you is the one you will enjoy. The institution that will be your spiritual home is probably next-door or around the corner. You may already have been there and found it imperfect or too expensive or "something." You might need to change it into what you need it to be.

Partnership lightens the load that almost no individual can carry alone. The load of life can be unbearable. It can be too much. And a lot of people won't even admit that it has become too much for them. They (we) are people who are ashamed of how heavy the burden is and how broken our back is. So we fake it. We act like we can carry a lot and then resent the fact that we have participated in breaking our own back, by not telling anybody we needed help.

If you want to renew yourself, or have something different happen in your life, ask somebody for help with something this Lent. And when they ask you in return, respond in the affirmative. That one question will change you and change your relationships. You will find yourself renewed if you can ask for help. You will stay the same if you don't ask for help.

Prayer: Holy God, you who have asked us to ask for help from you and from each other, give us a little gumption so that we can actually do that. Amen.

Action step: Try a new religious partner. Try a new group of people for your prayer group, book group, study group, after-hours entertainment. See what happens.

11. "When I was a child, I spoke like a child...when I became an adult, I put away childish things."
~ 1 Corinthians 13:11, Author's paraphrase

Renewable energy comes when we partner our spirits with our behaviour, our actions with our deepest hope. One feeds the other. Erik Erikson, the great psychologist, said that identity has a consistency over time. When we don't know who we are, we bounce around. Abraham Joshua Heschel said that life's largest and best task is to connect the inner self to the outer self. Maturity is spiritual consistency. It is a person whose insides match their outsides.

Mature people have what Paul Ricoeur calls a "second naiveté." We don't leave our joy behind so much as tend, befriend, and increase it in action. We are not always mature, but we know how to be so. We have that magic thing called executive function: we have changed our mind once in the last week. We have personal authority, which is nothing more or less than self-control. We know where we stop and others start. We don't take everything personally. We know how to say "thank you" when someone criticizes us. We engage in conflict and don't melt.

Prayer: Give us a second naiveté, a way to connect our child to our adult and be at one with ourselves. Amen.

Action step: Whatever hard task we have to do today, that task we call beyond our "pay level," imagine it as a joy, a privilege, an occasion for ecstasy. Stand in awe at how hard your day is. Give thanks for the difficulty. Let yourself be enchanted by how hard it is and then flow into resolution and the renewal of difficulty into enjoyment.

12. "Present your bodies as a living sacrifice..."
~ Romans 12:1

Daily life is one moment after another, when our actions speak louder than our words. We get to choose what happens to the world's environment and our own, minute by minute, hour by hour, day by day. Climate change is an accumulation of actions, not a one-time thing. Likewise, personal climate change comes by the simple choices we make. Day after day of eating trans fats will make us unhealthy. Day after day of not exercising will do the same thing. Day after day without the renewing relaxation of prayer will likewise add up to soul fatigue.

If we want the opposite of soul fatigue, our choices are simple. We sacrifice, daily, the harmful habits on behalf of the healthier ones. We don't say, "Tomorrow I'll get to that," so much as we say, "Here and now, I'll get to that."

Prayer: For the gift of me and my own weirdness, I say thanks. For the capacity to risk telling somebody else who I am and what I want to sacrifice, I say please. For the ability to turn towards the health I covet, I ask your help. Let me learn to distinguish the small from the large, the urgent from the immediate. And help me learn to please you, and to stop pleasing everybody else. Amen.

Action step: Find five words that describe the "you" you want to be. Make of them a short poem or a haiku. Give each of them a body part. Understand the word sacrifice, which means holy action. Make a holy action of your body. Redeem yourself. Resurrect yourself. Renew yourself.

Today, five words for myself might be supple, limber, liminal, funny, and fancy. Tomorrow they might be capable, secure, astonished, practical, poetic. Next week they might be lost, afraid, mixed up, scared, selfish. Another week they might focus less on my spine or my mind and more on my heart and how well protected it often is by my spine and my mind. Let there be a little tension in your five words. Let there be a little paradox. Make sure you don't always make sense to everyone who meets you. Make sure you're not pleasing someone else, but instead you and the God who loves and made you. Make sure you have a little mystery to yourself. That will be a holy sacrifice, a living body, wholly holy.

13. Jesus casting out the unclean spirit
~ Mark 1:21–34

Another redefinition of a health issue might help as well. Many of us can't renew or redeem because we are actually sick. We are already sick. Consider addiction. There is a sense of being inhabited when we are addicted. We don't need to go into "dirty" notions of bodies or anti-body thinking to reimagine a meaning for addiction. Addiction, many argue, is the inability to ask for help. What is remarkable about Jesus' encounters with people who say they have unclean spirits is that they know how to ask for help. And Jesus knows how to give it. Wellness might actually be the presence of ease and the ability to ask for help.

So many people tell me that they can't believe I preached a sermon about "blessing out" a hairdresser for mistreating me. I know I shouldn't have done it. I just lost it. The more we tell each other about our "losses," the more ease we will have. The more we let each other know that we are not perfect or even perfectable, the easier our constant renewal will be. We will return home to ourselves and discover that the unclean spirits are gone. We will resurrect, not once, but over and over again.

Please don't tell the drug companies that help is closer than we could ever imagine.

Prayer: O God, drive us to wellness, the wellness of asking for help, the wellness of ease. Help us to clean out our own homes. Amen.

Action step: Ask someone for help. Or try asking someone for help. Or get close to asking someone for help. You may not have the high class addictions of drugs or booze, but you probably have

something you can't manage, that has way too much control over you. Learn to say, "I need help," and to not be ashamed.

14. "He made the disciples get into the boat and go ahead to the other side, while he dismissed the crowds."
~ Matthew 14:22

August is the month when many North Americans take vacations. But you can vacate from vacations any time you want to, even during Lent, even on spring break. Any time you want to get away is a good time to vacate. And every time you vacate it is important to know the way home, too.

The sneaky truth about vacation is how much time "off" goes to what we will do or be when we get "on." We may say we "live for vacation," but mostly we don't. When we are "away," resolutions abound about when we get "back." New initiatives emerge. Four pounds disappear, no matter how much we eat.

Vacation means to vacate, to empty the place where we *were*, to be in another place. Vacation is one of the last few islands available for reflection now that so much of life is taken up with action or doing.

Jesus loved to vacate. He loved to empty. He loved to open up the space of the crowds and show them a way to reflective space, one where you can be alone but not lonely, apart but still in community, away from the moment while planning for the moment.

Like many of you, I loved watching *Downton Abbey*. My favourite line is when Violet, the Countess, asks her gathered brood, "What is a weekend?"

We may, of course, accept Jesus' imprimatur on our time "away," on behalf of getting "back." We may demand reflection on behalf of action. What is a vacation, possibly, when we love our lives so much that we don't want to separate from them? Or better yet, how, after this vacation, can the work we do in the world give as much pleasure as its opposite? Renewing ourselves for vacation while working? Or renewing ourselves for working while on vacation? Why not?

Prayer: Empty us, O God, into meaningful work and let us escape it as well, from time to time. Let us fully live and not just on vacation. Amen.

Action step: Evaluate your last three vacations, if you were lucky enough to have them. Do you need more meaningful vacations, or more meaningful work, or both? When what used to renew us no longer does, it is time to change. Find the power to change, even if it is just a plan to take another road home.

15. "Just then his disciples came. They were astonished that he was speaking with a woman..."
~ John 4:27

The successful entrepreneur who started the first "rent a chicken" company originally amused me. The concept was simple enough. It seemed to do some good. So many people want fresh eggs and their own birds. I have 12 of my own and was glad to see the yolky wealth spreading around.

Then I got involved in my sick jokes. Perhaps I should start a "rent a partner" company. Or a "rent a friend" one. Or "rent a child" or rent a "30-year-old son company."

It didn't take long for the word prostitute to arrive. And then it didn't take long to remember how often women are prostituted. The oldest profession, right? Where you rent a woman or tweet Grindr and get the kind of sex you want? You can buy eggs and you can rent chickens and you can buy sex.

Everybody knows prostitution is wrong and everybody knows it's common. Imagine how seriously my respect for Jesus grows when I realize that he actually talked to prostitutes. No wonder the disciples and the authorities were bothered. He didn't buy or sell, rent or joke. He talked to people.

New York City just did a million dollar fund raising campaign to improve the self-confidence of girls. It is all over the subway, in almost every car. I wonder what would happen if "holy" people talked to "unholy" ones. Self and confidence would become almost as good as a freshly laid egg. And each would be a bargain.

Prayer: Strange Jesus, we praise you for being different and for being so frugally moral while being so beyond morality. Help us to be the same. Help us learn not to pay for everything, but to be ready for gifts abundant. Amen.

Action step: Let us take a life inventory and figure out what we might be selling. Find a way to talk to that side of yourself. What are we renting and what are we owing? Give an honest answer to the question. You don't really have to tell anybody else if you don't want to. And from that fierce self-assessment, ask yourself what elegant simplicity might be possible instead. Get ready for a resurrection, using the pathways of renewable energy.

16. "Whatever you bind on earth will be bound in heaven, and whatever you loose on earth will be loosed in heaven."
~ Matthew 16:19

The most controversial subject in my congregation is the announcements, seconded only by joys and concerns. In these two worship instances, someone else speaks besides those hired to speak. Half of our congregation easily thinks the other half talks too much. Some people dominate the announcements or joys and concerns in such a way as to remove the holiness from them. If you speak every week, and others only speak every quarter, what does that mean? Self-congratulation or liking to hear the sound of your own voice both come to my mind. Neither is a compliment.

An announcement is an invitation to others to love something like you do. If you don't invite them, they won't know of your love and they won't know you. If you over-invite them, or compete with them for air time, they will not come. They won't really feel invited, but instead bound. And a joy is a joy is a joy. People know it when they see it and if you have one every week, good for you. A concern is very different. The pancreas of your second cousin twice removed is rarely important enough to take up two minutes of 60 or 75 minutes of collective time. Quietly suffering is better than talking if the injury is distant. Of course, if the injury is close, speak up.

What you say on earth matters on earth and in heaven. What you choose not to say also matters. Or more clearly put, what you do and don't do matters. Renewal and resurrection are choices we make about what we say and don't say, do and don't do, about when we stay quiet and when we speak.

Prayer: Help us, O God, to loose and bind, speak or hold our tongues, with a sense of community that manages our own egos. Amen.

Action step: Evaluate something that has long irritated you. Withdraw the permission for annoyance or change the behaviour or your participation in the behaviour. Lighten up. There is a negative energy afoot. And you don't really have time for it, or the spiritual budget for it.

17. "Jesus, full of the Holy Spirit, returned from the Jordan and was led by the Spirit in the wilderness, where for forty days he was tempted by the devil."
~ Luke 4:1

Only 40 days. Jesus was only tempted for 40 days. Most of us are tempted 40 times 40 days. In fact, we might argue that the Lenten experience of Jesus' temptations is minimal, if not minimalist. I am a maximalist about temptations. I have them every day, pretty much every time I put the key in the ignition of my fossil fuel filled car. Of course, I drive a Prius and am happy to excuse my participation in extinction based on that choice alone. I hope you are laughing at my easy way out of responsibility for extinction of the human race.

Now you think I have gone too deeply into the death that is always lurking during Lent. If so, just read Elizabeth Kolbert's excellent book *The Sixth Extinction*, if you accuse me of being overcooked about the environment. Hear her words. "At the risk of sounding anti-human – some of my best friends are humans – I will say that human survival is not, in the end, what's most worth attending to." She argues, as many environmentalists do, for the habitat, the soil, the community. In her previous work *Field Notes from a Catastrophe*, published after serialization in *The New Yorker*, she brought the perils of global warming to a large audience. Kolbert is an expert on the human crimes against nature. She also doesn't believe there was ever a time when humans lived more in harmony with nature. She holds humans responsible for multiple extinctions and doesn't even think it is that bad. Her kind of fatalism is just too easy for me. Plus, if the enemy is us, very few people will easily join the fight for the light. We are just too self-interested. I like to drive my car. I wouldn't know how to live without it. So I plan on being tempted to turn that key in the ignition for 40 more days and probably 40 more after that too. Curiosity, subtlety, nuance, self-possession, the ability to think and care are all casualties of the ecological debate. Many of us have a big curiosity about what is eventually going to happen. We have even learned to face our own powerlessness when it comes to nature. We can't help but use it.

When I offer you spiritual theories and actions for renewal and resurrection, I am not telling you that you can save the planet. Quite the opposite. I am telling you that you can't, and that you probably will drive a car anyway.

I have a dear friend who is just 70. Chinese-American, she is an artist and a paddler and can't find a job and has no retirement. She is astonishingly beautiful of face and figure and demeanour. She swears she is on her way to Hawaii to "go native," and raise pigs and chickens. I honour and applaud her. I think she might even do it. Do I think she will live beyond temptation there? No, I don't. She will still be angry at her last boss and angry that she has to leave her hometown.

People who want to renew and resurrect are especially interested in temptation and the truth about it.

Prayer: O God, when we imagine that somehow we can turn to the good and live in the light, take us back to the wilderness and reacquaint us with the devil. Amen.

Action step: Read Rebecca Tuhus-Dubrow's "Endgame," in *The Nation* magazine (July 21/28, 2014). Ask yourself if you are part of the problem or part of the solution. Get to know the devil. There is no reason to imagine that resurrection is easy. It is not. It happens after you meet the devil and death, not before.

18. "And whoever will not receive you nor hear your words, when you depart from that house or city, shake off the dust from your feet."
~ Matthew 10:14, KJV

Bill Keller, former editor of *The New York Times*, said, as he retired, "If 80% of life is showing up, 20% is knowing when to leave." You may shop for a spiritual home. You may live aware of your own complicities and of your own devils, who fully tempt you. You may have friends and communities that accompany you on your way. But, someday, you will come to a place where you have to unpack your bags. You will have to say, "I live here and not there." You cannot keep changing and renewing. In fact, often the way for genuine renewal is to come to terms with where you are, as well as *who* you are. Renewal is placement. It is living in a place, as if we belonged there.

Many of us left our spiritual homes of origin for very good reasons. They bored us, ignored us, hurt us, and confounded us. It may be time to go back and it may be time to move on. But if you don't practice with a people, you will find yourself very alone.

If you don't settle on a place, the earth will never know the care of built soil and affection, which happens when you start where you are. Religious institutions "hatch, match, and dispatch." They accompany us and our children in rites of initiation like baptism or *bris*; they connect our partners to us, in weddings; and they become our last location, in funerals and memorials. Sometimes Lenten renewal is as simple as paging through a photo album and taking the time to remember dates and times, people and places. An odd version of renewal is looking at the faces of the people who are no longer alive. In remembering, we can renew. What kind of renewal comes from communing with the dead? We begin to question that straight-line view of life and go into cycling. Not just recycling, but cycling. We know life is a circle of connections, like a labyrinth that reaches all the way back to the Grail in its tendrils.

When people don't have a "folk" way to initiate, connect and leave, we become powerfully lonely. The text about shaking the dust off your feet can be read in a couple of ways. First, it can mean shake the dust off against the people of the town. It can also mean shake the dust off and stay awhile. You probably won't find a perfect place or a perfect people. But you can become an improved imperfectionist. I try to become a better imperfectionist every day about my office without a window, or my house that has a leaky basement. I try to love their dust. After all, it is *my* dust.

Prayer: Help us, O God, to have not just a spiritual home, but a real home, in a real place, with real people. Help us to renew our appreciation for what we have and who we already are. And then help us to improve, imperfectly. Amen.

Action step: If you are one of the many who are always thinking about moving, or at least de-cluttering the place where you live, make a choice. Move. Or stay. Or de-clutter. But don't think any more about doing those things. Just do one. And then congratulate yourself. You will have defeated the spiritual tax on everyday life and will live tax free. You will have a decision. It will renew you.

19. "Remember the sabbath day, and keep it holy."
~ Exodus 20:8

We live in a pervasive time famine. Time has been stolen from us and we haven't even chased the robber out of the house. Here follow five ways to keep a Sabbath, especially for people who don't have time to keep one. When we don't ritualize our weeks, we homogenize time. Without a Saturday or a Sunday or a Friday practice, a way to keep Sabbath and to interrupt time, we are sitting ducks for a culture that only knows Starbucks as coffee and has no problem turning us all into photocopies of each other. People who are religious in spiritually practical ways retain their "original." They find their original. They have folk and they have folkways. They know the back roads and are not on the interstates all the time. They know their place in such a way as they come to know their time. They renew a sense of time and place every chance they get. Sabbath is that renewal. You can keep a Sabbath ten minutes an hour every day all day long by the simple art and act of goofballing when no one is looking. Think of your sit spot. Sit in it. If you can't get to your sit spot, make believe you are in it and close your eyes and see what you see of it, by way of your imagination. Second, you can keep a whole day off the grid, off the machines, detouring the Internet. Third, you can say a prayer before one meal every day.

A long prayer. A real prayer. If you don't pray, just keep your mouth shut till you start filling it. Fourth, you can cook a meal every Friday for the people you love the most and light a candle with them. You don't have to get the Hebrew right. Fifth, you can take a Sabbath every third Tuesday, whether you need it or not. You get the picture. Lent is not the only time for a Sabbath practice, but, without it, even Lent will pass you by.

Prayer: O God, make of us Sabbath keepers and not just in Lent, but for a long time. Let us learn how to rest, especially if we have forgotten how to. Amen.

Action step: Add a sense of prayer to all the practical suggestions in this devotional. Pray to be able to Sabbath. Connect the practical to the spiritual and know that sometimes the devotional is the practical and the practical is the devotional. Confuse the spiritual and the material as often as you can.

20. "Be still, and know that I am God."
~ Psalm 46:10

It was Frances and Jacob's wedding, at Lake Atitlan in Guatemala. Jacob and Frances had gone to Jesuit internships together, where they unsuccessfully tried to save the world. (Now Jacob is a tenant organizer and Frances an immigrant rights organizer.) Frances was Chinese-American and Catholic; Jacob, African American and Unitarian. Their parents were all still married, which is remarkable in itself. Funny part was each couple had been married 41 years. This wedding started off like so many, saying, let's leave God out of it. Which is, of course, impossible.

You can try to find renewing redemption and recycled resurrection without God. But it will be a lot easier *with* God, or with a partner like God. Don't worry about becoming religious! It won't hurt you. Call God "Spirit" or "Force" or even just "energy," beyond the energy you already have. Give God a nickname if you must, the way my daughter-in-law has named her bicycle Francesca, or I named my cancerous breast Lola. Make up a name for God. Ask her to be your mode of transportation. Or your imaginary friend, like the kind children have. Whatever you do, don't defensively try to keep religion out of it. If you are too wounded by what religion has done, unpack that defence. Do you also think government should be abolished because of what it has done or hasn't done? Do you also imagine that anything that is tarnished can't have value? What about you, you who have lost your lustre as well?

Prayer: Help us to find at least one name for God and stick with it long enough for it to wear out. Help us to outgrow one kind of religion after another. Amen.

Action step: When you become embarrassed by God or by your feelings towards God, imagine a spiritual approach you haven't tried yet. Amuse yourself by how urgently you are in search of a renewable energy that recreates and re-creates you.

21. Faith the size of a mustard seed
~ Luke 17:6

The next big idea is the big idea that the next big idea is a little one. Bigness is killing us. Smallness releases us. You may have picked up this book because you wanted to find a way to be renewed or

resurrected this Lent. You, like many of us, really wanted to be different. You wanted to change. You wanted to be transformed. You wanted a different set of aches and hopes, possibilities and probabilities. Maybe you wanted to learn to be happy with a little change, instead of the full totalitarian variety.

You should meet some of the people I know who think the practice of yoga is only good if you do it *every day*. When I tell people I do a little yoga and have my own custom practice, they get wide-eyed. "Every day?" they ask. And I tell the truth. No, not every day. When I can. Maybe three days a week. Do I share their disappointment about my lack of regularity? You bet. I would love to tell you that I am an everyday yogi. I am not. My posture shows my postures and how infrequent they are. Same thing applies to my church: we have grown too big. We need to get small again. Small is beautiful. Less is more. Fewer is finer.

The same smallness and irregularity applies to what we believe about God. Maybe Lent is a good time for a shakedown. Do you think you need to fully believe in some version of God, along with some magnificent worshipping community of fellow believers? How big does your God have to be? And did you ever think of being kind to yourself and being glad that you can believe in some kind of Spirit, some of the time? What would happen to you if you started trying to be small, with all the effort you are now putting in to being big? Might you not be born again?

Prayer: Tame our spiritual ambitions, O God. Tame our practices. Tame our big ideas. And then train us to see the "lot" that is in the little. Amen.

Action step: Think about what you could get rid of. Think of how you could release on the matter of growth. Could you be smaller, less successful, less numerical? Who are you trying to please anyway? What would happen if your church capped its growth at 200, or your budget capped its growth at $50,000 a year? Then what? Just imagine for a while what it would mean not to be the slave of growth. You could put the "unused members" on a waiting list, the unspent money to another family who needs it.

22. Workers in the vineyard
~ Matthew 20:1–16

Jesus always spent more than he had, always paid forward, always had a strange understanding of the economy. The workers in the vineyard? The story where the one-hour worker gets the same as the eight-hour one? Jesus is anti-labour and anti-capitalism in the same breath. Jesus was a self-emptier, a kenotic, one whose way was to spill and spend, not hoard and scrimp. I have no idea if he would vote to limit debt or to increase it, but I do know he would frame the entire argument in a way no one else does. What will the orphan or the widow get out of it? One of the things it means to love Jesus is to be pro taxes and for frugality. In other words, reframe the question. The way the subject is reframed will be good for either orphans or widows, and will proceed to means from these ends.

Jesus spoke up without having full solutions to all problems. The deficit would not threaten him so much as engage him. He would push us to resolution and not to dilly-dally around, as though someone else needed to help the children and the aged, the orphans and the widowed. These are metaphors for spiritual abandonment and economic loneliness, as well as for material need.

Jesus spoke on many levels at once, and wasn't afraid to open his mouth. Spiritual renewal is a gorgeous thing. Lent is also a gorgeous time. Without renewed care for those who are oppressed, it won't have much spirit to it. With that renewed care, it will overflow in new ideas and new ways of looking at things.

Prayer: As we become new, release us from self-obsession and enter us into the world where we dare to care for those that few people care about. Amen.

Action step: Today, find someone you don't need to care about, or smile to, or even notice. Notice her. Care about him. Give them a smile. Find out who is more refreshed – you or the person to whom you have connected unnecessarily.

23. "If you have eyes, see. If you have ears, hear."
~ Matthew 13:16, Author's paraphrase

There are times when I just can't think of another thing not to say. Prophets tell truth long before people want to hear the truth. Prophets tell it long after people have heard enough, too. Prophets tell people more than they want to hear. Jesus spoke with a singular disregard for long-range planning and solution-oriented programs. He was stuck on the simple verbs: see, say, hear. When we don't see or say or hear, we turn our words into orphans. Orphans cause cruel silence. Orphans and widows were the beginning, the end, and the middle of Jesus' understanding of the problem we have with our common senses. When we see or hear or speak, we adopt the orphan, the one inside us and the ones we don't yet know.

Jesus helps me deal with political polarization as well. He spoke the unspeakable. Love your enemies. Be good to those who hurt you. That means I need to love the those who hurt others, who I would just as soon murder. (Not all, just some.)

Now, I do have some squabbles with this too-good-to-be-true man/God. Did he really not want us to have power? Or victories? Or self-worth? Yes, he probably did. But he also understood the importance of self-emptying, of *kenotically* giving those things away as often as possible. For Jesus, the way out of mutual demonization was the way inward and the way inward was the way out. He didn't have or make time to demonize. He kept moving us towards a centre in each other – while driving us out of our comfort zones. Like a labyrinth, he was always trying to head for the mountains, always at the gate of the city, always afraid of the centre. He knew the church would throw a homeless person off the pew, even during a worship service. He knew good Christians would find a way to convince themselves that documentation is an important thing when people cross national borders. The Jesus I love is a gatekeeper, not a border control guard. He gives us the possibility of a centre in each other by throwing us off centre and outside so we can see the so-called "other" as a mirror of our most inner self. Let us learn to be quiet with the poor and with their mirror of us.

With the Jesus I love, I also learned a quiet that I didn't know could be. There is brevity to Jesus' speech, a calm to it, a near non-chalance that keeps me from babbling in the Babel. He doesn't say much, but he says enough. He notices, he re-centres and de-centres. He prioritizes the poor.

How did he achieve this equipoise, this rare blend of action and peace? By making God, the one he called *Abba*, his priority and from there noticing the poor. For some people it is uphill both ways.

Jesus loves these people especially. Most congregations, including mine, could learn to love Jesus' people more – the ones who snore during service, whom others call lame or retarded, whose feet hurt from waiting on tables, who get molested in hotel rooms, whose roommates photograph them having sex, whose only life is a beer on the 5:47 train after a long day of bosses and boredom. We could so easily have half the programs and twice the impact, if we stopped being afraid to touch the wounds, and the wounded. The programs so often take "staff," which distances ordinary people from other ordinary people. Programs count how many we have "served." *Renewed* people count how many people they have touched. Their numbers are smaller and their impact is larger.

Prayer: O God, when we ache for renewal, acquaint us with grief so that our renewal can rebound and redound. Don't turn our renewal into a "should" about the poor. Instead, let us *sit* with them, *see* them, *talk* to them, and *turn* their "them" into an "us."

Action step: Spend the day focusing on your common senses, the ones most people have. See. Hear. Smell. See what happens if you bring into consciousness what your common senses show you.

24. "I have come to make all things new." "Behold I make all things new."
~ Revelation 21:5, KJV

There are so many dead ideas that walk among us like zombies. We act as if nation states were God's idea of a good time, as if homeless people are the cause of their own homelessness, as if people should

be paid what they are "worth." This latter zombie idea somehow ends up with some executives getting paid more than anybody could ever be worth, while other people's unemployment cheques run out long before the next one arrives. Why? Because the widows and the orphans are not prioritized. Jesus' ideas are the opposite of dead. They are different. They are unsettling. They prioritize what we ignore and give us a centre in each other, and a way out of using the word "other" at all.

Then there is the matter of hope in the future, something I usually refer to as my increasing political pessimism and despair. Jesus is risen. He is the only Messiah who never really shows up, intentionally, I think, in order to keep us with something to do, to keep history open, to avoid the rigidity of the right, which imagines that God stopped speaking right after the last psalm was written. For better or for worse, Jesus really meant it when he said we were his hands and his feet.

Spiritual renewal comes when our hands and feet have the *oomph* of the new and have let go of the stale. Spiritual renewal shows up in our overflowing capacity to love those whom no one else seems to love. Some call this Christ-like. I call it the Jesus way. No matter your words, Spirit-led people are renewed, renewing, and renewable, and not just for themselves.

Prayer: Guide our feet while we run this race, so we don't have to run this race in vain. Amen.

Action step: Give yourself a manicure and a pedicure. If nothing else, just stick your hands in water or your feet in a bucket full of suds. Think about how important your hands and feet are. Imagine what you would do without them. Remember the last time you had plantar fasciitis, or the first time you will have it. Stand in awe at a God who made you a partner. Note that we become new by awakening our hands and our feet.

25. "No longer Jew or Greek... male or female..."
~ Galatians 3:28

One of the most stale and least interesting ideas around is that of gender. Spiritually renewing people are just about always bending gender. We are always wondering what our gender means, or what somebody else's gender means. We aren't afraid of gender, but instead fascinated by its multiple forms. We don't say, "Because I am a woman, such and such follows." No, it does not. "Because I am a man, such and such follows." No, it does not. When we find the energy we need to be renewable, redeemed, and resurrected, we usually have to walk through some kind of gender door. "Oh boy, you are having a girl," we say, with all the humour that implies.

Jesus also has an uncanny way of bringing me to the matter of gender. He was clearly queer, if by queer we mean that spacious place beyond gender's chicken coop. He was un-gendered, or at least didn't seem to care about his masculinity. As our own culture faces a crisis of masculinity, one so deep that it shows up in all the sit coms coming out for the fall, Jesus, the champion table turner, would argue that we also face a crisis of femininity. We can't blame the capitalists or the union, the Democrats or the Republicans, the men or the women. Jesus turns that table, first by reframing demonization, and then by driving the demons out and our own goodness in. With Jesus, you can't even have a good enemy, or an easy answer, or even a fancy well-considered answer, or a gender binary in which to hide from your true self.

One day, and it didn't last longer than that day, I painfully realized that I didn't like my father, and I didn't like my husband, and I didn't like my son. And, what my deep disappointments in my intimates meant, was that I didn't like myself. I didn't know how to love those who weren't what I wanted them to be. Jesus showed me a way, a way beyond worth. They didn't have to be what I wanted and needed them to be in order for me to love them, or for them to love me. This insight was worth decades of psychotherapy. It even drove me to a curious form of non-partisanship. Oprah is not the only one who understands women's deep disappointment with men and men's deep disappointment with women. These matters start with the prison of gender, which Jesus managed to ignore.

Prayer: Renew our sense of gender. Open us to transitioning, as a life practice. Amen.

Action step: Have a conversation with someone you know well enough to enjoy a risk with. Ask them how it feels for them to be masculine or feminine. Tell them what it means to you. Refresh your ideas of gender.

26. "The fruits of the spirit are love...kindness...self-control...and gentleness."
~ Galatians 5:22, 23

Jesus' kindness is so often confused with weakness. But, in fact, it is the only strong thing I know in a world that is trying to make me weak. Every time the news reports said this was "Endeavor's last launch," I thought they were talking about my morning. Turns out they weren't. Jesus' love re-launches my hope.

Once, my husband was very unhappy about something that had happened. I touched his cheek with my hand. He wept. I didn't know that I was kind, or had the capacity to be kind. I do.

Once, I had to tell my college chaplain a terrible truth about me. He knew I had come to tell him something important. He met me at the train station. I had my gloves in my hand as I got off the train. He took the gloves out of my hands and put them on me. Then I told him what I had to tell him. He said, "Oh, no." And after that he said, "It's all right."

One of the fruits of the spirit is gentleness. We need it. And we can give it. It is amazing how renewing it can be to go gentle into a tough world.

Prayer: When we don't think we have the capacity to be kind or gentle, help us to be wrong. Amen.

Action step: Think of yourself as someone in search of a low-cost form of personal entertainment. Imagine that you are in charge of solving the appreciation deficit syndrome. Make a small touch, a handshake, a look in the eyes your objective. And see what melts in you and in others.

27. Shout for joy, sound the trumpet
~ Psalm 81

I have a problem. Maybe you have some version of it, too. The problem is that there are an increasing number of matters on which I have no comment. Worse, I have nothing to say. Not just nothing to say that hasn't already been said. The problem is worse. It is a kind of spiritual and conversational isolationism. Let's nickname

it "quietistic quiet." The topic of Gaza comes up. I go quiet. The topic of police violence comes up. I go quiet. The topic of Colony Collapse Disorder, fondly nicknamed CCD so you don't have to hear the word collapse, comes up. I go quiet. I go into horrified, quietly.

You see, I have a habit of speech. Problem? Solution. Trouble. Fix it. Quietistic quiet is breaking my habit.

In my family, we really can't talk about Israel or the Gaza strip. My son and daughter spend most of their time fighting about it. This summer has been all about the two-state solution and the way Israel is destroying Judaism. Yup. You may think Israel is thousands of miles away. It is not. It is in my car, at my table, and in my emails, many of which start with "What are you going to do about her?" Or him? Or them? Instead of the two-state solution, I want to discuss the two-sibling solution. But I don't and I can't.

I hope to renew my quiet before Lent ends. I want it to be a different kind of quiet. One that doesn't embarrass me, but consoles me. One that doesn't accuse me, but assures me. When I don't have anything to say, why not say nothing? I know we are told to shout for joy and sound the trumpets. But when we don't do anything but babble, why not go quiet? Eventually that quiet will lead us out of quietistic quiet into the real thing.

Prayer: Release me from my own Tower of Babel, O God, and move me out of my own babble. Let me find words that are worth saying, and help me say them. Amen.

Action step: I want to recommend a Lenten practice to you. Don't say anything when you don't have anything to say. Stay in the quiet. Spend a day or two talking as little as possible. Tell your friends and your family that you are going on a trip to the land of quiet. Unpack your bag there. Dust your feet there. Stay a while. When you are ready, come out. Your speech will be renewed.

28. Shout, Sing, Listen
~ Psalm 81

If you have read this far and are still looking for renewal and resurrection, hooray. You may also be reading this far and wondering where the solutions are. That would also be good. Here's a tip. There are no solutions to renewable energy except renewed energy. Sometimes renewing energy takes you to odd places, like reading a psalm such as number 81 and realizing that its verbs are really different than the language of pattern and problem (unsustainability and low energy) and solution (renewable energy, resurrected).

The lyrical language of Psalm 81 is full of promises, most of which God has not kept. Israel will be free of its enemies. Nope, not this week. The land will flow with milk and honey. Nope, not this century. The moon will rise. Well, at least that happened last night.

I know the names of many problems. I even have nicknames for some of them and real names for the rest. What I don't know is what to say, how to fix, how to resolve. Moreover, I am not sure God *wants* me to fix or resolve. God wants me to *sing* out loud, to *shout* with joy. To *raise* a song.

The Psalms use a pattern of speech that is not problem/solution. The word that helps me most in Psalm 81 is "would." God says, "I would feed you with the finest of wheat, and with honey from the rock I would satisfy you."

Because of this promise, I can dig my fork into the soil with new resolve. I can speak but not in the problem/solution way. I cannot use the speech of fix. Instead, I use the speech of shouting and singing and listening. These verbs are different. They receive the promise and then wait. They understand the threat and then re-state the promise.

Prayer: O God, change the way I read and think, the way I shout and sing, the way I fix and don't fix. Amen.

Action step: Read Psalm 81. Notice the verbs. The next time you start giving advice about how to fix something, stop in your tracks. Remember the African who told the missionary, "Please just stand in the mud with me." From there, stand in the mud for a while. At least you won't be exhausted from failure. You might even find the Jesus way to connect with those who have failed, only to fail again.

29. "For God so loved the world..."
~ John 3:16

For me, renewal is often as simple as remembering how small I am and how large the world is. Then I can relax. God has the whole world in God's hands, thereby removing its burden from my flimsy shoulders.

While in Italy recently, I was newly impressed with the musicality of the Italian language. *BerGAMo. Radicchio. Grazi. PREGO.* The Italians are always speaking like they are so terribly excited about everything, even the fact that you just ordered a coffee.

I went to the World Frisbee Tournament in Lecco, Italy, where my son's team, which was supposed to win, lost. We lost by one

point in the semi-finals to the Japanese team. One lousy point. It was Jacob's last tournament because he has aged out and is now off his team. Your youngest son (a) is not supposed to turn 30, and (b) is not supposed to get cut from the team he used to be captain of. I am on my way to talking about much larger injuries here but, needless to say, I felt this one. And I couldn't fix it either.

You may not know enough about the game of Frisbee. You know it is played with a round disc, but you had no idea that some people actually take it terribly seriously. Did you know that it is the only sport where men and women, girls and boys can play on the same team? Did you know that there is an award given for "spirit" as well as for winning? The team that gets the spirit award gets it because they have played nicely with others and because they had a good spirit. Did you know that, at worlds, each game ends with a circle of the opponents, alternating members of the opposing teams? For about 90 minutes, the teams battle each other fiercely up and down the field. Then they hug and shake hands, and give gifts and tell each other stories about their home country. My son's team beat Prague, then Croatia, then Venezuela. They went on to beat Toronto and Moscow. Then along came the Japanese. Our men from Boston were about a foot taller than the Japanese players. There were times when it looked like they were running through the legs of our team members. The game has no referees and decisions about fouls are made by talking. Yup, talking on the field. They get to speak, they get to play, then they hug, no matter who wins or loses. The game depends on turns. One team sends the disc down the field, the others score. The game stays even till someone makes a mistake, a "turn," and then you have a chance to score two in a row. This conversation is often delightfully non-verbal at the international tournaments because yes, the Japanese

speak Japanese and the Ukrainians speak Ukrainian. At the tournament, which is played on a polo field, it only rained two days, thus bringing up the delightful manure smell of the earth below our feet. There were 64 teams playing on 32 fields. The flies were especially prominent in the big tent, where we bought sandwiches and beers between games. There was always entertainment in the big tent and it wasn't just swatting flies. A chamber orchestra played most afternoons after lunch. Three women painted three other women, brush to body. The painters wore clothes; the models did not. Others thought they were mocking selfies, which mock the portraiture of the rich. I think that was overthinking. I think it was some kind of joke about the Italians, the portraiture, the music, and the colours. We couldn't stop staring. There are about a dozen groupies attached to each team, mostly parents. We stand out because we aren't wearing uniforms or treaded shoes. And we are not 20-something and oddly not part of the 20-something culture. Thus, when we took photos of the nude paintings, people thought we were weird. Perves.

Toward the end of the week, the chamber orchestra changed to a Klezmer band. Needless to say, I was renewed. How? I saw how big the world is and how small I am. I became reacquainted with my "speckness" in a way that made me feel large and grand.

Prayer: O God, when you tell us you love the whole world, send us with a spirit of receptivity. Help us not to need a referee, so musical is our language with each other. Amen.

Action step: Go someplace. If you can, go someplace far away. Love it.

30. "Keep watch over the door of my lips..."
~ Psalm 141:3, KJV

You may also be wondering about your tongue and how to use it well, and not just during Lent. Learn the Hebrew word for tongue; it is *Lah.shon.rah.* It appears over and over in the psalms and scriptures, where there are multiple messages about not gossiping, not telling secrets, not going into triangulation. Interestingly, nowhere are we told to go out into the world to fix it. Instead, we are to *listen* God's promise into being. The worst thing about the fix-it pattern of speech is how distancing it is. How self-justifying it is. You can be sure you're misusing your own tongue if most of your language is self-justifying, solution-based, smarter-than-thou.

Fix-it speech distances you from other people's trouble and from God. God *"woulds"* to walk with us in our mud; with our enemies, internal and external; and to hear our song of gladness over milk and honey, honey bees and combs.

Let me give you one example of different speech. The subject of Colony Collapse Disorder came up at a party I was at last night. One of you was there, or at least you have been at one of these parties. Instead of the morose silence of the quietistic Donna or the fix-it tsk-tsking, you might say, "I saw a bee just yesterday, right here." Hear the song in that? The promise in that?

Speech is something we all use all the time. Pointing to the promise is better than fixing the pain. And sometimes the pain is fixed by a promise!

Prayer: Help us to be the people who use our tongues to point to the promise, over and over again, so thoroughly that even the bees hear us and return to the work of making honey. Amen.

Action step: Give thanks that you can speak, that there is a gate that opens and closes when it comes to your mouth. "Watch your mouth," and watch what it says. Let it become alert for what is buzzing.

31. "God's hand is on the flint and overturns the mountains at their roots.
God cuts out channels in the rocks......"
~ Job 28:9–10, KJV

The poet Louise Bogan says that the surest way to still poetic talent is to substitute an external struggle for an internal one. This passage drives you to the internal struggle between you and God's promises. It drives you there. God has a fix. You don't. God has a promise. You don't. God has a prayer. You don't even have that, if you are a self-justifying fix-it machine. Get over it. Get on with it. Collapse the winning part of the hive that is you and get to the Spirit part. Then you can get back to the music of the game. Tunnel all the way through the rock God made. See all its treasures.

On our way to Lenten renewal, there are many external conflicts. Time. Money. Energy. The people who have disappointed us and who may disappoint us again. Finding language poetic enough for these external conflicts is a form of renewable energy. It redefines. It gives a new name. It opens up the windows in the rooms. It lets the door ajar on the places of captivity. Time can be tended. Note the shift to a verb orientation. We can tend time. Money. Why would we think we needed to have more money to have more energy? Just the reverse is possible. The more energy we have, often the more money we have. And the more we are able to ignore the money we don't have. Disappointments. Yes these are frequent, common,

everyday, and maybe even perpetual. We can rob the time we have free from them by fearing when they are going to come again. We can tax the good time with worry time and therefore let worry have the victory. Or we can experience the disappointment as it happens and refuse to give it forecasting power. We can move on. We can let go. We can live in promised time, not polluted time.

Just finding the internal language for the external problem? I don't call that just. I call that poetic.

Prayer: Turn us into everyday poets, O God, and help us to refuse to substitute an outer struggle for an inner one. Return us to our outer struggles with fresh vigour, renewed energy, and a point of view on the next one. Amen.

Action step: Name the inside part of every outside problem you have. Embrace the shake of your hand with your inner and outer self.

32. "But if through my falsehood God's truthfulness abounds to his glory, why am I still being condemned as a sinner?"
~ Romans 3:7

This is one of those Pauline-type questions that contains a trick inside it. Like its more famous partner, "What then, shall I sin more so that grace may abound?" the trick revolves around the matter of cheap or inexpensive grace.

Cheap grace is when we count on God to forgive us so much that we persist in sin. Sin can be defined in many ways. Here I mean it as "missing the mark" of our true humanity. We lower the

bar God has set for us and imagine that God's overwhelming love for us is such that we may as well have another drink, or cheat another client, or forget another homeless person's name. Cheap grace tosses us into the hell of relativity, where we sense a deep inconsequentiality about our lives.

Rich grace, the kind that shows up in the coin of changed behaviour, is so moved by God's anyway love for us that it begins to live on a different planet, a different plane, a different plateau. Instead of thinking that what we do doesn't matter, we know it does. We are almost driven to show others what it means to be secure. We are compelled to be different than what we were, so drawn and magnetized are we to the high bar of true humanity. It is not so much achievement, although saved people do achieve, as it is lighting up on all of our cylinders, where before we were only showing one or two bars. Instead of being burnt out, we are lit. Instead of being sad, we are happy. Instead of being bored, we are engaged. Instead of being frozen, we live in the unfreezing stage, pretty much all the time. From fixed and rigid, we become flowing.

Prayer: Help us to enter the divine mystery of You, O God, and help us get over being expert about God. Help us clear the room and the way for something interesting to happen. Amen.

Action step: Sustainability is the capacity to weather what's wrong with us and also the capacity to be wrong and to *know* we are wrong. We know we can be wrong. We are not afraid of being wrong. We are only afraid of getting stuck there. Right one wrong in yourself. Right one relationship. And let that become a habit.

33. "God split rocks open in the wilderness, and gave them drink abundantly as from the deep. God made streams come out of the rock, and caused waters to flow down like rivers."
~ Psalm 78:15–16

One of the organizers of the Washington, D.C., Occupy movement came to a national meeting of faith leaders at our church three days before Christmas. She was 75, a former self-described "lieutenant in Dr. King's army." She said that the Occupy movement had turned her into water and she just felt poured out, so reinvigorated was her hope for human right, and human rights. She said she felt like we had another chance to make our mark as a democracy. She said she had remade a decision that she had made a long time ago. She used these words: "What I do really does matter."

Cheap grace drives you to inconsequentiality. Grace drives us to consequentiality, not the kind that makes us self-important so much as the kind that pours out, overflows, gets everything that was all dry all wet again. We are *not* to sin more so that grace may abound. Just the opposite: we are to make our mark as creatures of a God who was not fooling around.

As bodies, we are more water than not. What if we became more water than not as spirits?

Prayer: When we are tempted to devalue ourselves, gracious God, drive us to the deep grace that is the well of our wells. Amen.

Action step: Go to a stream and sit by it. Or find a stream online, or a recording of flowing water. Sit by it. Let its flow become your flow.

34. "Let the rivers clap their hands; let the hills be joyful together..."
~ Psalm 98:8, KJV

Many people say they find God in nature. God *is* in nature. God is also in traffic and in driveways, available on Sundays and on Mondays, on mountaintops and in ditches. God refuses all captivity, even by sunsets.

Sometimes I clap my hands to get people's attention. I don't have a big voice so I use other methods. I know how to clap my hands in appreciation, too. In fact, I probably do a lot of clapping.

I don't think hills or mountains or floods can really clap their hands, although I know what the psalmist meant. I sometimes feel like clapping when the New York sky turns that cobalt blue that it showed on 9–11 long ago. There is a beauty to that blue that marries the Hudson River's grey and the Atlantic's azure.

When I think of becoming a more sustainable person this Lent, I think of my wonder at the blues and greys of my hometown. I think about how much I love them, so much so that I feel like clapping. I wonder if the river and sky are clapping, too. I wonder if we are in this together?

Prayer: O God, keep my hands able to clap, keep my spirit deep in appreciation for what is all around me. Let me not quibble with the psalmist about whether hills can clap, but instead enjoy the amusement of the idea. Amen.

Action step: Go outside sometime and just start clapping. See what happens to your spirit.

35. Entertaining angels unawares
~ Hebrews 13:2

Spirit is often found in all the "wrong places." We frequently are unaware that we are surrounded by angels.

Spirit can even be found in a religious institution, in ritual practice. But Spirit will surprise you. You can count on that. Many confess they have looked for God in all the wrong places. Scavenging is a spiritual strategy that opens up space for God to find you. Scavenging may not seem like much of a spiritual practice, but it is actually an excellent one. It gets us into the deeps of the lost-and-found department, and not just in the airport. It causes us to understand what it means to be once lost and finally found, in the words of the great hymn "Amazing Grace." It allows us to have more than one identity.

I love shopping in thrift stores because they don't identify me as one type of person. There I can try on the costumes of a skinny girl or a plump matron or both. I can imagine the maternity clothes as having been just right for that period of my life. I can experiment with colour and size, and see the whole world on the racks, row after row of identity options. Fashion may not be your thing. And the prices of expensive clothes may not be your thing. But surely you want to entertain some options. Surely you want to imagine that an angel is lurking right there in that same old, same old you. The one you have become bored with, the one who doesn't even interest you sometimes.

Scavenging is one of the most green things in the world to do. It keeps us out of stores. It keeps us in good clothing that has already depleted the environment in its making. It also patterns in us the possibility of surprise. Spirit will come as a surprise. Why not scavenge as a rehearsal for it? We might even scavenge in a church.

There is always lots of dust there – and not a few angels.

Prayer: O God, keep our eyes open for what has been left behind and abandoned. Keep our hearts open to leftovers. Keep our habits green and let us learn how to be spiritual scavengers. Amen.

Action step: Go to the deadest church you can find and try to worship there. See what happens to your spirit.

36. "These are the generations..."
~ Genesis 25:12, KJV

Spiritual renewal will involve all the normal things of our lives. Probably. But be careful to involve them too much. Whatever our base of operations, and even if we are single and live alone, there are some who will be known as our family of origin. These relationships are holy, even if they are sometimes broken. How to be a family member as a spiritual and religious person is important. We are not alone. We have been bent into shape or bent out of shape by our people of origin.

Some like to brag about their ethnic origin. Others are ashamed of it. Still others don't care about it, so vanilla have they become. We are a part of seven generations before us and seven after us. To be truly sustainable, we will have to recognize that and become a grandmother who had a grandmother.

Our family tree is important.

Prayer: I pray for my mother and my father, my sister and my brother, and all who came before me and all who will come after me. Amen.

Action step: Draw a family tree and see what it tells you. Let the tree speak to you.

37. "Pray without ceasing..."
~ 1 Thessalonians 5:17

While prayer may be a constant practice, it is also true that life is large and long. Details and domesticity intervene in ways too numerous to mention. Prayer helps us practice letting go. It imagines never being "done" or "finished." Like homemaking or raising children, prayer is a highly domestic activity.

One of my favourite homemaking tools is the scissors. Scissors help. I'll show why. They declare what is enough for today. Scissors help those of us old enough to have lost some of our grip. They get us into packages that appear at first sight to be impossible to open. I think of the plastic that surrounds the ear buds I just bought. Scissors help us choose what part of the picture we want to keep. They cut out the excess and keep what we want to save. They also help us read the newspaper and act as though we want to keep something from the news of the day. Scissors clip. They are decidedly against everything at once. They are in favour of selection. The spiritual practice of selection keeps us on target to do what we can do and not do more than we can do. I like to clean my house in a circle, by which I mean attending a part of it each day, one corner at a time. That way I don't think it is ever done. It just keeps gathering dust. And I keep flowing into sections and selections of order.

Spiritual practice can be the same thing. Some days are good for a prayer of thanksgiving, others for a prayer of confession. Why not choose what is sufficient for the day?

Prayer: O God, when we feel that life is chopping us into little pieces and we wonder if maceration is our middle name, come close enough to remind us that we are choice-making beings. Put some scissors in our hands. Amen.

Action step: Take the biggest project you have and break it into small pieces. Pray each piece. Then go into action. You will find that you can write a novel if you write three pages a day, or clean out your house if you do a corner a week.

38. Maundy Thursday

When you eat the sacred meal tonight, imagine that it is your last supper. Eat it with gusto. Eat it with people. Look around the table and realize that everyone at the table is also trying to renew themselves and is as intent as you are about living in a sustainable way. Know and acknowledge that part of you that has seen capitalism meet up with climate change in the big-systems way, and in the small spiritual way that your own heart quakes and aches for good things. Imagine disruption as a good thing, for you and for all of us. Pause during the meal. Disrupt its gobble. Enjoy its grace. Play or sing that great mysterious song, "Take a Load Off, Fanny." Make a good joke about your load and the burden everyone carries. Really imagine that small is beautiful, that less is more, that fewer is finer. From that sustaining place, challenge the systems that are deep inside you and all around you. Challenge the internalized capitalism, and the kind that shows up in your paycheque and on your time sheet.

Try to do the right thing in the right way, rather than just doing the right thing. Risk being wrong. Enjoy the change. Remember

that great press advice: It's not the crime. It's the cover-up. Uncover your secrets. Take them out to play. Don't blame the system, but instead blame the way the system showed up at your table in its food and its social arrangements. From there, make a decision to blame no more but instead to celebrate what is. When you do that, you will sacralize all that has been desacralized. You will live free from lies, and free for truth.

It can all start at the last supper, the Passover table, the table that passes you over to the other side.

Prayer: Grant me Grace at Table, O God; today, tomorrow, and ongoing. Amen.

Action step: Take no actions for the next three days. Let these days be your holy days. Let them hollow you out.

39. Good Friday: "You will know them by their fruits. "
~ Matthew 7:16, KJV

When good things come about because you are in the room, it is possible the Holy Spirit has been with you. The opposite is also true. During Lent, we seek the Holier Spirits and the Holy Spirit. We try to make the positive go viral and to keep the negative from air, wave, and airwave. We are mightily aware of the difference between good and evil, especially on Good Friday, when another good man is put to death for no good reason. Both life and death can go viral within us. Today, of course, we experience the humiliating and senseless and violent death of Jesus. And we make every vow not to let that death be the last word, or to let its reality go viral in us. We promise ourselves that we will not let evil invade our spirits.

Consider the purple loosestrife. It is a lispy thing. It is an invasive species of marsh plant. It actually looks beautiful in bloom. But the plant is demonic instead of spirited as follows: it goes rapidly into a monoculture, knocking everything else out, cattails and rush, even salt hay. It uses a monoculture to mess up a system. It also changes the way water flows, and destroys the food sources for many marsh animals, especially turtles. A plant can have over a thousand seeds, which adhere to clothing and are very pointy in their seed sack (looking like a Halloween kind of devil). There is an antidote to loosestrife: the Galerucella beetle, which is even smaller than a loosestrife seed.

When you are gone from this planet, will there be more of a monoculture or more biodiversity? Will you have crowded out native plants or learned to live among them? Will there be more turtles, more slow things, or fewer? Will you have changed the way water flows and, if so, will the flow help more people or hurt more people? Will you have increased the food sources or decreased the food sources available to people?

Prayer: Let our spirits be invasive in earth-opening ways. Let them fruit. Amen.

40. Holy Saturday: The Strife Is Over, the Battle Won
~ Hymn title, revised

Spiritual and religious people honour creation as a reflex action. We know earth and sky as home. I have a full-moon book. It is one of my most precious possessions. Every time I see a full moon, no matter my location on the planet, I record it. I have a record of all the moons I have seen for the last 15 years. Yes, like my yoga practice, I skip sometimes. I forget to record, or I miss the moon's rise altogether. Sometimes the moon is obscured by the clouds. But for me, there is a great allure in the archives. And a great love of place, even though my places change a lot.

Spiritual and religious people are joined at the hip of nature and history. We love material life *and* spiritual life – both, not either. The weather with us is usually good, even in a blizzard or a hurricane, even on a subway or a bus. For spiritual and religious people, the world is a whole, not a bunch of parts. We are connected to the moons and to nature's multiplicity of features because we imagine God is active there. Climate-scorching hurts us especially. Why? Because we know God speaks in thunder. We also know that valleys will rise up and mountains will come low. And we understand that even thunder is threatened.

Naomi Klein has written an important article. Called "The Change Within," in *The Nation* (May 13, 2014), the essay argues that something called capitalism is at war with something called the climate. We know this within our hearts, but we don't really know it yet. We will, after the next tornado typhoons, or the next Sandy silts. For now, let me summarize her argument.

Climate change demands that we consume less, but being consumers is what we know. Climate change is slow, and we are fast. Climate change is place-based and we are everywhere at once. Climate pollutants are invisible, and we have stopped believing in what we cannot see.

Klein swears she is not judging us or blaming us, but instead helping us to recognize that we are products of an industrial project, one intimately and historically linked to fossil fuels. She asked Wendell Berry for advice and he said, "Start where you are. Love your home place more than any other." But what about rootless people who live on their computers and who always seem to be shopping for home? "Stop somewhere," Berry replied. "And begin the thousand-year-long process of knowing that place." We would begin by remembering the generations, those as far back as we can go and as far forward as we can imagine. Thus, we "home." Thus we "revise." Thus we find the future. Here, month by month, we record the moons we see.

Prayer: O God, when climate change scares the bejeebies out of us, help us to remember the generations and to slowly home, hone, and revise our plans. Remind us often that the strife is over and the battle is won. Amen.

Easter: The women ran from the tomb, afraid but filled with joy.
~ Matthew 28:8, Author's paraphrase

E. B. White, the famous writer of *Charlotte's Web* and more, found his wife, Katherine, a brilliant editor at *The New Yorker*, in the last year of her life, dressed in her business suit while placing daffodil bulbs gently into the Maine ground in November. She was "calmly plotting the resurrection," according to White. She knew she was sick, she knew she didn't have long, but she did have hope. Surely she was afraid. But she wasn't afraid enough to resist planting.

She reminds us of those women at first discovery of the empty tomb. They were surely afraid, but not enough to preclude their hope or joy. We begin the Lenten cycle with a destination in mind. We, too, want to find the tomb empty, or at least *some* tomb empty. We are willing to weep, as long as joy comes in the morning, or to the next generation of bulbs or people. We believe in the 7th generation, even if ours is gone.

Michael Piazza, a new church planter, spends a lot of time asking people to let go of old ways of doing church. Perhaps another time than 11 a.m. on a Sunday, the time the youth we covet like to sleep? Or stand-up meetings around tables in a café style, so that people can actually talk to each other rather than "take" "Minutes"? Hard fights that happen without Robert's Rules and perhaps instead use Roberta's? Mike says, with feeling, "Help me plant a church for your grandchildren."

This Lent may we calmly plot the resurrection; one bulb, one person, congregation, and one day at a time. Amen.